Acknowledgments

Heartfelt thanks to Amy Beeker, whose vision brought this cover to life with color and joy, and to Becka Hall, whose keen eye and design talent brought harmony to every page. Your creativity and dedication have turned a fun dream into a reality, and I am grateful for each hour spent and detail.

Dedication

For my son, Mac...

May you know that being strong means being true to every feeling, big or small. Boys can be fierce and brave, but they can also be soft-hearted, silly, and filled with wonder. I love you!

A is for AHHHHH

I feel overwhelmed.

B is for BOOHOO

I feel sad.

C is for cuddly

I feel like being held.

D is for dazzling

I feel like a star!

E is for EEEP!

I feel so excited!

F is for Fluttery

feel like I have butterflies.

G is for GRRR

I feel mad.

H is for HIP HIP HOORAY!

I feel like cheering others on!

I is for ICK

I feel sick.

J is for jumpy

I feel scared.

K is for KEEN

I feel eager!

L is for lollygagging

I feel like being a jokester!

M is for MERRY

I feel so happy!

N is for neighborly

I feel like a good friend.

O is for ooh-la-la

I feel fancy!

P is for PHEW

I feel relieved.

Q is for QUIET

I feel like listening

R is for Rawrrrr

I feel like letting noise out!

S is for Sleepy

I feel like I need a nap.

T is for TA-DA

I feel like I want attention!

U is for UGH

I feel bothered

V is for VICTORY

I feel like a champion!

W is for WOW

I feel surprised!

X is for Xoxo

I feel like giving hugs and kisses!

Y is for YAY!

I feel like confetti!

Z is for zing!

I feel like I have an idea!

www.ingramcontent.com/pod-product-compliance
Ingram Content Group UK Ltd.
Pitfield, Milton Keynes, MK11 3LW, UK
UKHW061030310726
14089UKWH00009B/177
* 9 7 9 8 3 3 0 3 5 0 5 9 9 *